HOLD ONTO HOPE

Practical Tips to Harness the Magical Power of Hope

Dr. Carol Stockall MD

USAGE RIGHTS

LIMITS OF LIABILITY AND DISCLAIMER OF WARRANTY

WARNING – DISCLAIMER

ACKNOWLEDGMENTS

I give great thanks to the people in my life who have been my personal beacons of hope in my private life. I am grateful to the people who have shared their struggles and shed the light of hope into my professional life. Your hope has been contagious. You have helped my own hope to shine a whole lot brighter. Thank you!

DEDICATION

To everyone who has lost hope and struggles to find it again. My hope is that this book and these tips help you find the hope you need to not just survive but thrive.

ABOUT THE AUTHOR

People often search for solutions during times of suffering. Carol has firsthand experience seeking solutions for the suffering of her patients, her clients and herself. Hope is always her first step in healing suffering.

Carol Stockall is a caregiver who has worn many hats. She began as a candy-striper, and later became a nurse, doctor, coach and counselor. A lifelong learner, Carol has a host of academic and professional letters behind her name including; BA, RN, MD, FRCPC, ACC, MC, and CCC. With decades of professional health care experience combined with a lifetime of personal experience Carol has earned a "PhD in life" that only comes with experience.

Today Carol's most known for her work coaching and counseling caregivers. She is a professional coach, certified by Erickson Coaching International, the International Coach Federation and the Physician Coaching Institute. Carol holds a post-degree diploma in Interprofessional Mental Health and a Master's degree in Counseling. Her thesis work was focused on burnout with a special interest in mindfulness to build balance and restore resilience.

Carol is dedicated to helping people hold onto hope and live out their life dreams. Get Carol's **FREE JOURNAL** to help you hold onto hope, download it here now at http://carolstockall.com/hold-onto-hope.

.

Use the journal as a companion to the book and jot down notes as you read. Then you'll be on your way to a brighter future.

To connect with Carol, visit her website at www.CarolStockall.com. Carol offers coaching and counseling for caregivers. Whether you are a caregiver in your home or at work connect with Carol and explore her list of helpful resources to help you hold onto hope.

TABLE OF CONTENTS

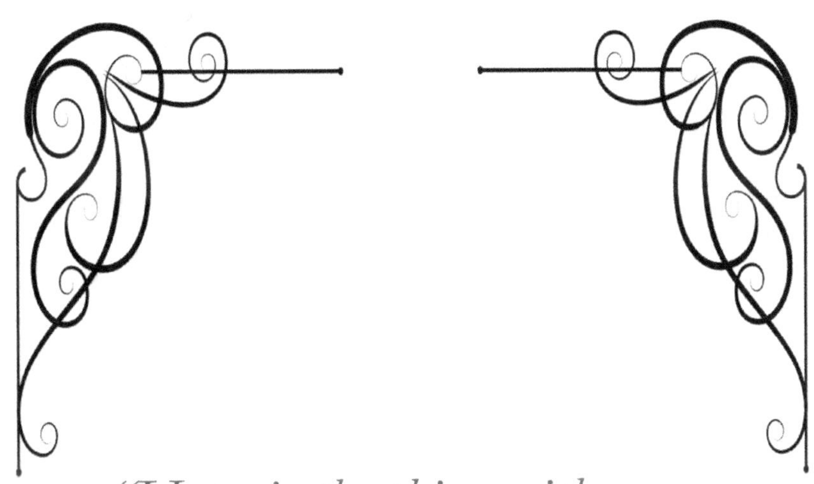

"Hope is the thing with feathers that perches in the soul and sings the tune without the words and never stops at all."

~ Emily Dickinson

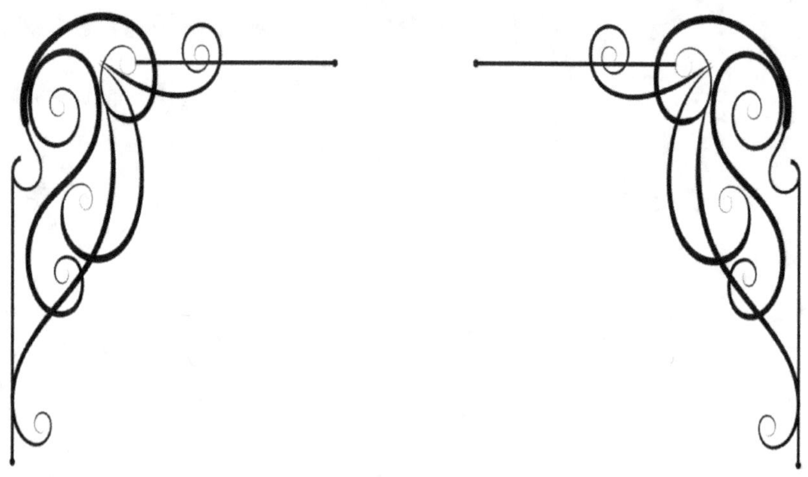

"Hope is the wind beneath
your wings."

~ Carol Stockall

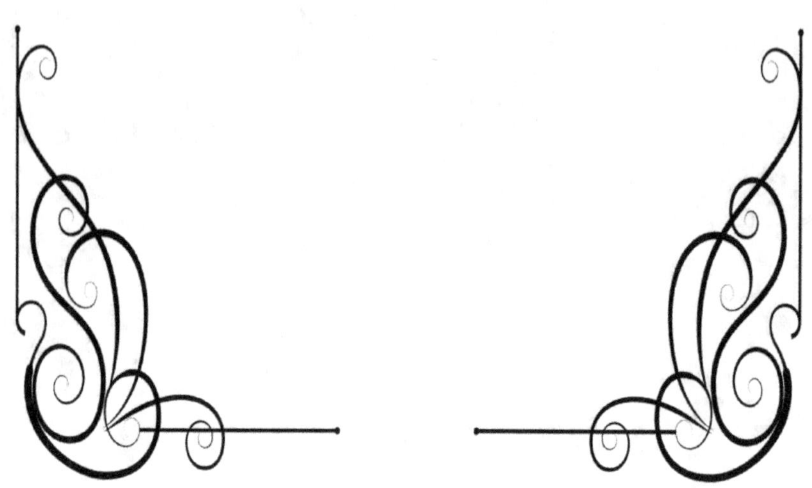

WHAT IS HOPE?

Hope is one of those things that people don't always understand well, though oddly enough, we all need it to live a happy, healthy life. After all, hope is gives you the courage to face your problems and search for solutions.

Hope is a feeling. It's an expectation and desire for a certain thing to happen. Hope sees the potential in a situation. But it does more than that. Synonyms for hope are; desire, wish, and dream. Hope is about anticipating positive outcomes.

Hope isn't some warm fluffy bit of happiness, nor is it a Pollyanna dose of enthusiasm, though it might contain both emotions. Instead, hope is a goal that includes both the desire to get there, and the feeling that you can.

The thing to realize is that hope is necessary to live. Without it, you not only stagnate, but you also lose our will to live entirely. You fail to thrive. Hope matters. Hope is the power that encourages you to push through the pain of adversity and thrive in spite of your struggles.

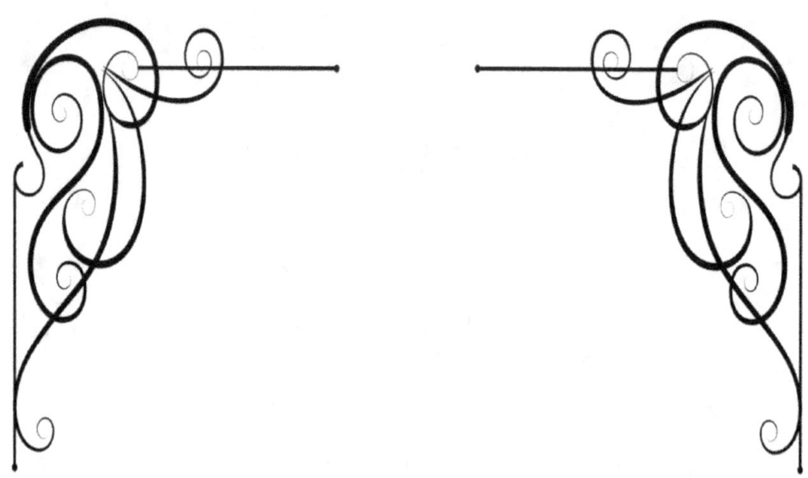

"Hope is the sunshine that gives you the energy to blossom and flourish despite the darkness."

~ Carol Stockall

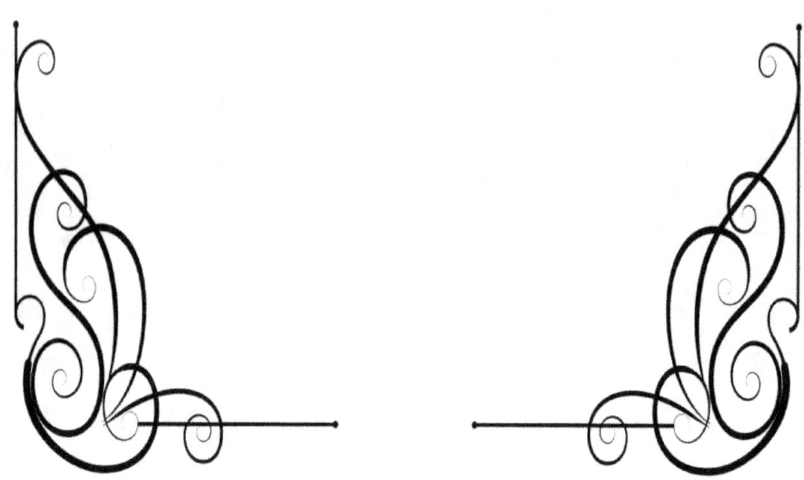

WHY HOPE MATTERS

Hope gets caught up in the interconnectedness of things. You need hope to realize your dreams, but as a group, our communities likewise need hope to survive. Everyone helps everyone. Hope shows you what we live for, and what you want to fight for. Hope has four big benefits.

1. Hope makes you creative.
Without hope you wouldn't go hunting for out-of-the-box solutions to your problems, nor would you waste time trying to find a new way to do things.

2. Hope puts you to work.
Without hope, there's no point in even trying to get a project done. Hope tells you to get to work and pushes you to keep going, even when enthusiasm starts to fade or when obstacles arise.

3. Hope pushes you past any failure.
With hope, you can see your setbacks as opportunities to learn and grow. Hope ignites your problem-solving abilities, so you discover a better way to do things through experimentation and persistence.

4. Hope makes you look toward the future.
More than that, it helps you let go of the past so you can welcome a bright future with open arms. Hope imagines a destination, and then helps you get there.

What's the best part about hope? It's contagious. If you go out into the world full of hope and enthusiasm, you can be sure to find that reflected at you by those around you, by those who have learned how to hope because you first showed them the way. Hope obeys the laws of attraction.

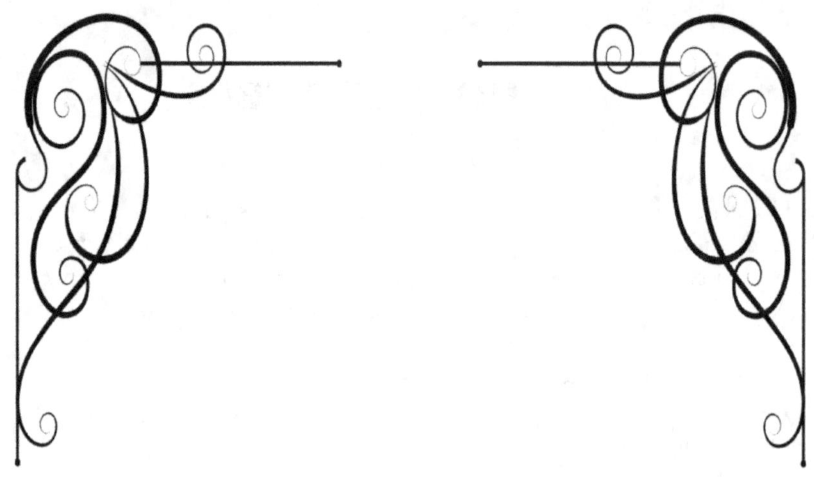

"Hope is the emotional
oxygen you need to survive."

~ Carol Stockall

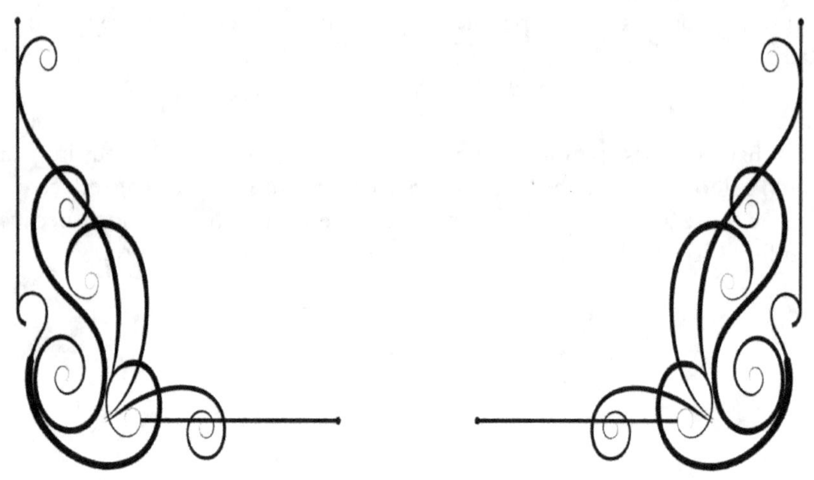

TOP 10 REASONS WHY YOU NEED HOPE

Hope. Without it, you sink into depression and despair. With it, you can set on a path of self-discovery that leads to the realization of your dreams. With all that, it should come as no surprise that the hope within you matters. Here are some more reasons why you need hope:

1. Hope keeps you from falling into a downward spiral of despair.
Despair thrives on negativity and will always point you at the worst possible outcome. Negative thinking is a trap that pulls you down into a dark hole that can be hard to climb out of. It's your hope that enables you to see a brighter future, filled with possibilities. Hope helps you climb out of the pit of despair.

2. Hope enables you to learn the lessons in failure.
At some point everyone is going to fail. While it's easy to wallow in disappointment and use it as an excuse to quit trying, hope refuses to give up. Instead, hope demands that you look at failure as an opportunity to learn.

3. Hope keeps away useless, negative emotions.
When you are willing to let in a little bit of hope, it's possible to balance the sadness and fear that would otherwise overwhelm you.

4. Hope gives you the nudge you need to learn something new.
When you feel hopeful you set goals. The tricky part can come after—when you need to learn new skills before we can even set out to pursue your goals. Hope is what moves you forward and gives you the willingness to grow and stretch beyond your comfort zone.

5. Hope keeps you trying.
Without hope, there's no point, and we give up planning a brighter future. Hope strengthens your muscles of perseverance.

6. Hope is healing.
Studies have shown that people who have cancer have better survival rates

when they experience hope. Hope is a powerful physician! Hope is a prescription that's good for everyone.

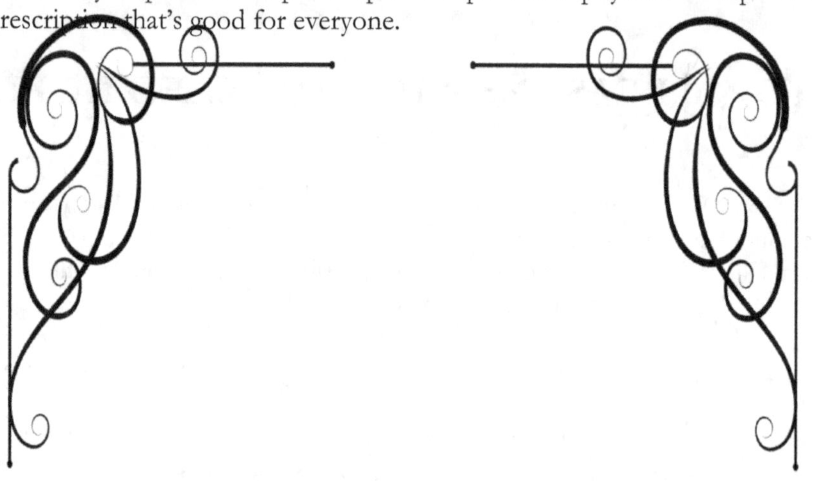

"*Hope is the emotional energy that inspires action.*"

~ *Carol Stockall*

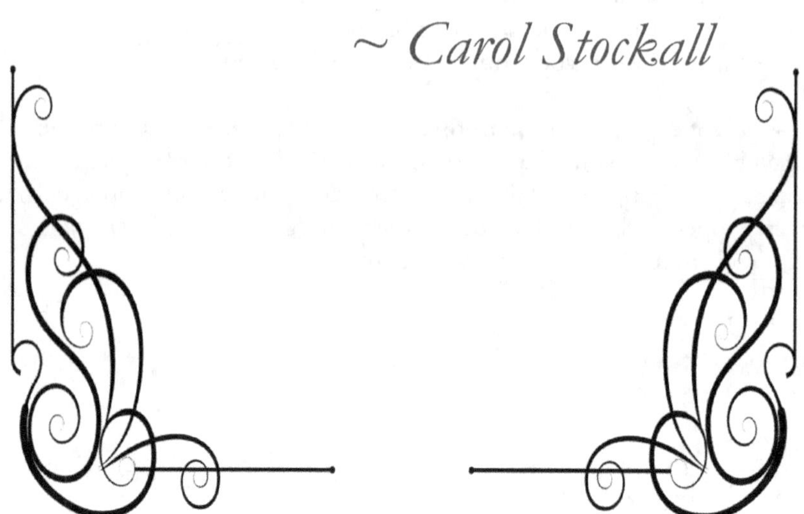

7.   Hope enables you to laugh.
When you're in the dumps of despair, nothing is funny. Hope allows you to relax enough to be able to laugh even when times are tough.

8.   Hope connects you to the people around you.
Without hope, you isolate, preferring to hide away from the rest of the world. Hope is what drives you to get out, mingle and do things. Hope is an antidote to social anxiety.

9.   Hope enables you to see a positive future.
Hope spots the potential in a situation, even the most difficult times. Hope sees the light in the darkness like the stars in the night sky.

10.   Hope brings about that bright future.
Hope is a wish that becomes a dream and develops into a plan. Hope is visualizing your goal destination before you even begin. Hope imagines the roadmap and it's the lantern that lights your way forward. Hope puts you on the starting line and smiles at you from the finish line. Without hope first, you'd never know success at all.

With all the benefits of holding onto hope and all the ways even a little hope can improve body and mind, it's easy to understand why the saying "never give up hope" is such a powerful mantra.

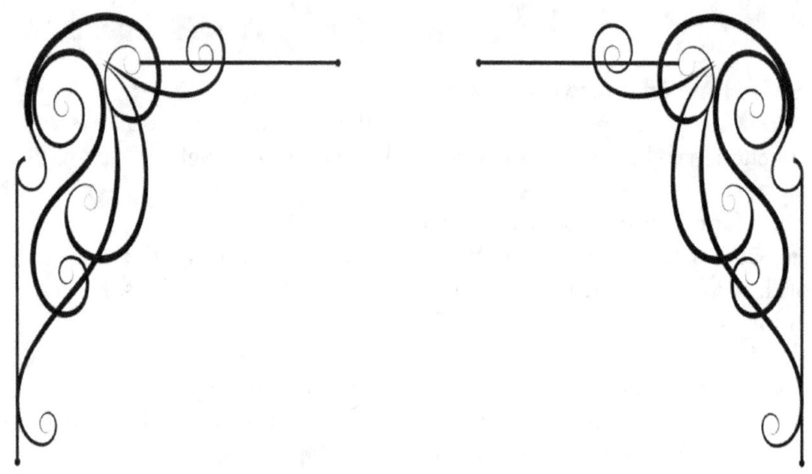

"Hope is always everywhere; you just have to keep looking for it."

~ Carol Stockall

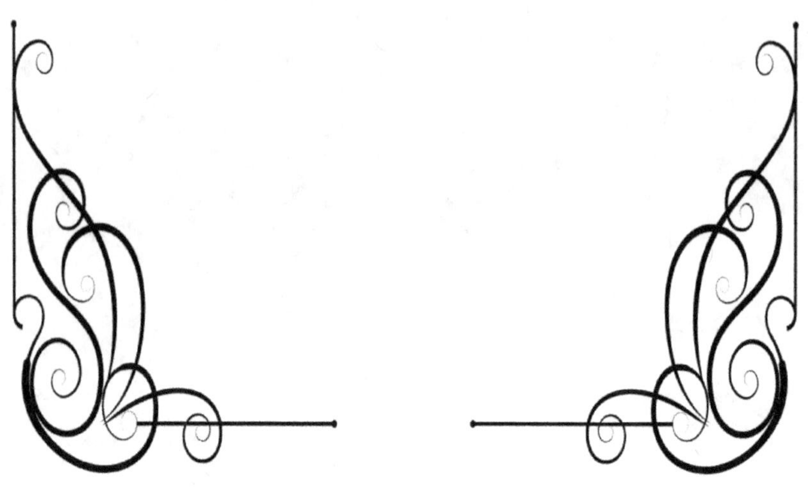

PLACES TO FIND HOPE

Without hope, you struggle to make even the smallest headway towards your dreams. When the worst happens, you need hope more than ever and sometimes hope is in short supply when you need it most. If you are struggling to believe that things can get better, take heart. There are several places to find the inspiration to rekindle hope.

1. In Action

If you have a goal but don't seem to be moving ahead on it, you can find hope in taking action. Despair and depression are born of inaction. The longer you put off making a move on your goal, the less hopeful you will feel about ever attaining it. Action changes everything. Once you take that first small step, your fear will fade, and you'll experience the feeling of hope once again.

2. In Others

Opening up to others, telling them your feelings and letting them know your needs enables them to likewise reach out to you. Our brains are wired to crave connection with our tribe, and when we allow that connection to take hold, our tribe can inspire us and offer hope in a limitless number of ways. When hope seems lost ask for help, or get professional help.

3. In Giving Hope to Others

When you share your time, energy, and resources with the world around you, you become the hope in the lives of other people. Spreading hope is one sure way to guarantee it's around when you need it. Sharing hope is a message of kindness and compassion. Service to others is a sure way to spark hope in your own life.

4. In That Small, Still Voice

By listening to your intuition and follow its guidance, you will discover hope in unexpected places. Even if what your gut is telling you seems impossible, go with it. You will find hope at the end of where it leads you. Take time to listen to your inner wisdom.

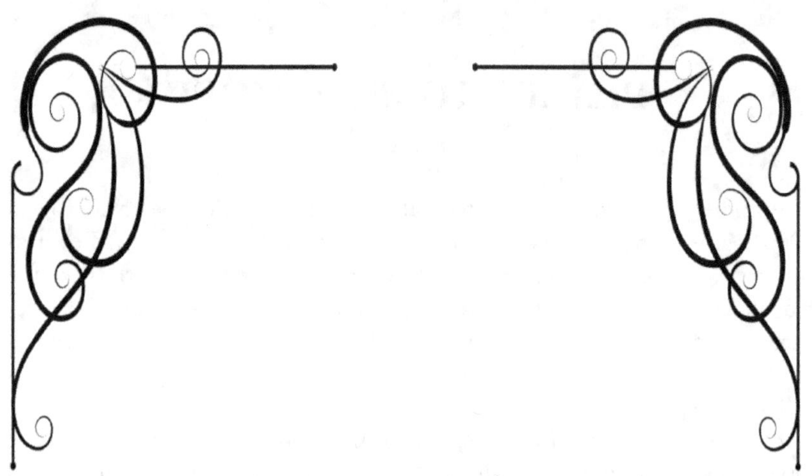

"*Find hope in the darkness
by looking for the stars.*"

~ Carol Stockall

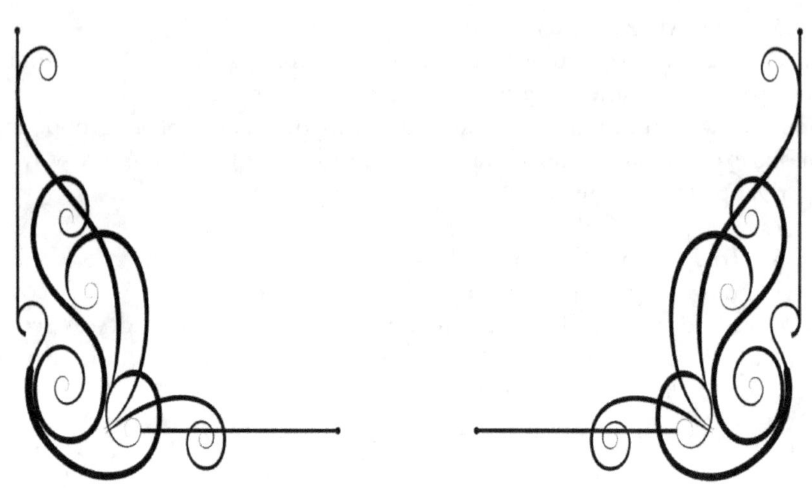

5. In Saying Goodbye to Old Baggage

By letting go of the negative influences in your life and the things that hold you back, you leave room for hope to grow in its place. That includes everything from decluttering objects that no longer give you joy, to finally putting an end to relationships that leave you drained and broken. Once you let go, you'll feel lighter and more hopeful than ever before.

6. In New Knowledge

When you are always ready to learn something new, you open yourself up to possibilities you wouldn't have noticed otherwise. This process shows you what you're capable of and guides you toward a future you wouldn't have had otherwise. Hope hides in every lesson learned.

7. In the World Around You

Look to the people who are doing great things, who are bringing positive action and change to the world. These are the people who give hope by just doing what they can to make the world a better place. Take inspiration from them. Ask yourself what can you do today to improve the world so that tomorrow looks a bit brighter?

Remember that hope is always available. Hope is everywhere. But you have to look for it.

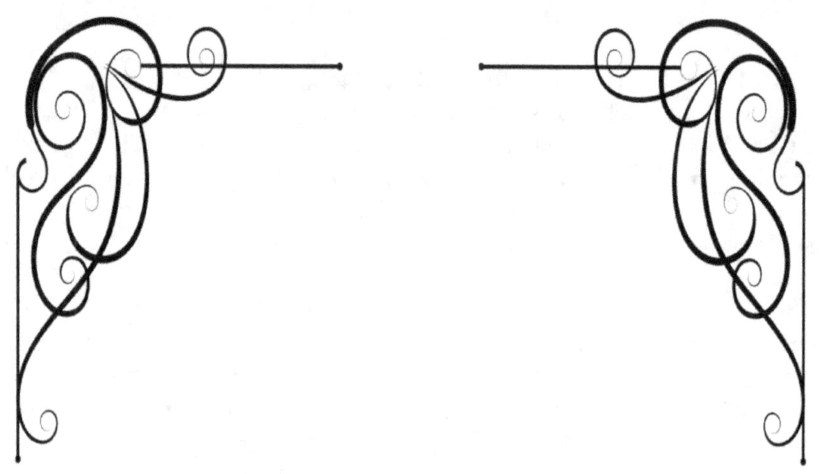

"Having hope gives you the
stamina to survive your
struggles."

~ Carol Stockall

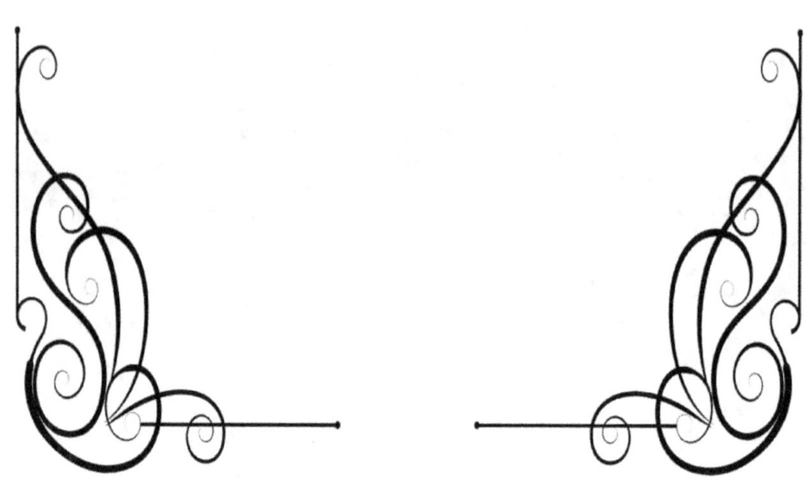

HOLD ONTO HOPE
DURING TOUGH TIMES

Struggles are inevitable. No one escapes difficult times in their lives. Whether you like it or not, your life challenges teach you the most. The ability to stay hopeful during those tough times is a skill, and one that is well worth developing. Here's how you go about holding onto hope.

1. Accept the challenge for what it is.

If you've been hit broadside with a difficulty that's left you negative, the worst thing you can do is try to ignore that it's there. By acknowledging the problem, you can deal with it head on and find a solution. Start by asking yourself if the issue is something you can change. If so, then it's time to make a game plan. If not? Then learn how to live with the new reality, rather than wasting time and energy fighting it.

2. Ask yourself what you can learn from this experience.

By seeking out the lessons to be learned, you can calmly face the problem. Discover what you can about the situation, learn, let it go and then move on.

3. Revisit the past.

You've been through tough times before. Think back to them to remind yourself that challenges don't last forever. Hope springs up from the knowledge that you've gotten through problems before and you can do it again.

4. Record the experience.

Blogging, journaling, or recording what's going on helps you to process the experience and find creative solutions. Putting pen to paper is especially powerful When you get things out of our head and onto the page, you're able to deal with problems logically rather than emotionally. Looking back at your own words becomes a powerful story of your journey. Your progress as you process the pain becomes an inspiration of hope.

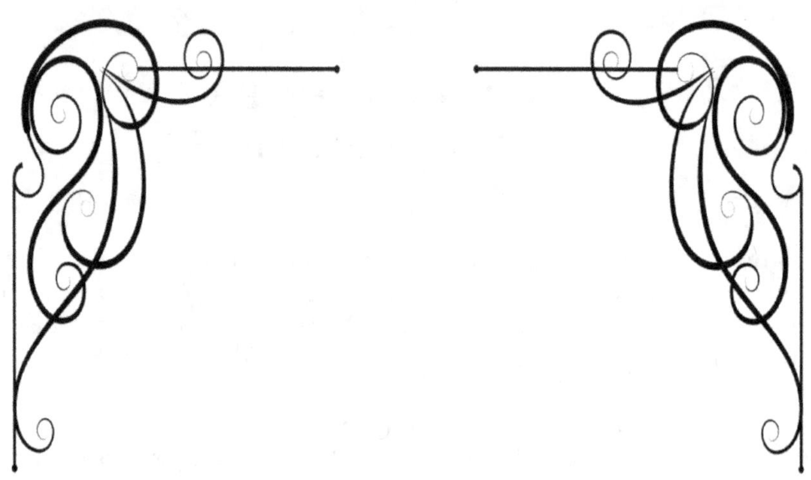

"If you have hope that tomorrow will be better it makes today's hardship easier to bear."

~ Carol Stockall

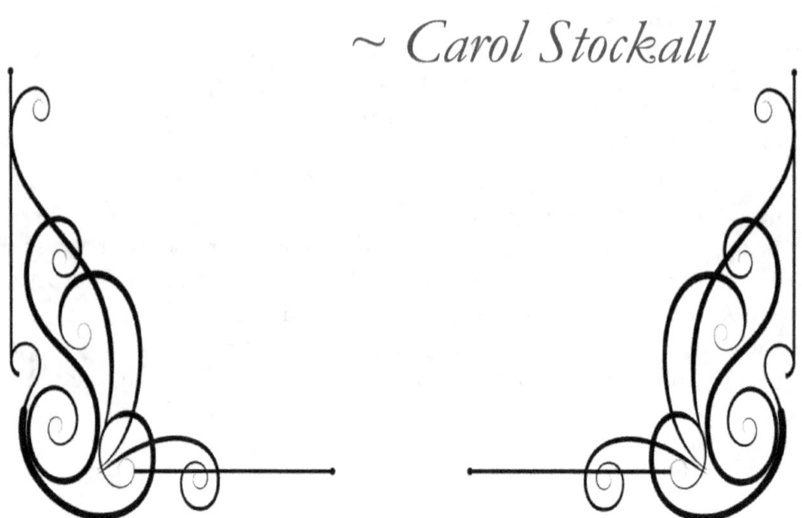

5. Laugh.

Even if you don't feel like it initially, the act of laughing changes moods. Hopelessness doesn't stand a chance against a good belly laugh. The fun thing about laughter is, once you start, it's hard to stop. You can even fake it till you make it with laughter. It will lighten your mood and help you see solutions that weren't there before. So takes some time to laugh out loud.

6. Choose Happiness.

Much of your life can be spent 'shoulding' on yourself if you let it. When life becomes a series of 'shoulds', ask yourself instead what you want to do. As long as it won't hurt others, make the choice that will create happiness in and then watch hope flourish.

7. Build a support group.

Trying to manage tough times alone is a sure recipe for hopelessness. Gather people around you who make you feel hopeful just by being with them. By spending time with positive people, their hopefulness will quickly become your own. Everyone needs support in good times and bad.

Hope is a constant reminder that time changes everything. Nothing lasts forever. Hope helps you remember that just as the good times come and go the hard times don't last forever either. Hope helps you hang in there until something changes for the better. When you feel like quitting hope helps you remember why you started.

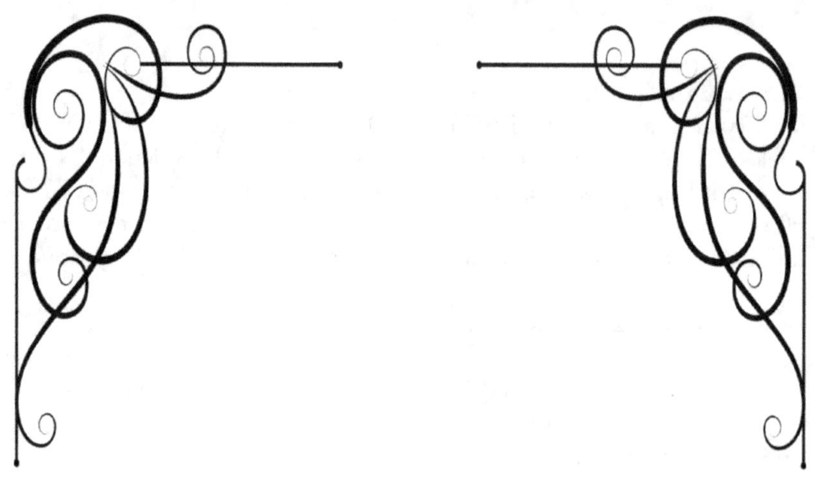

"Sometimes mere chance
brings you better luck than
you could ever hope for."

~ Carol Stockall

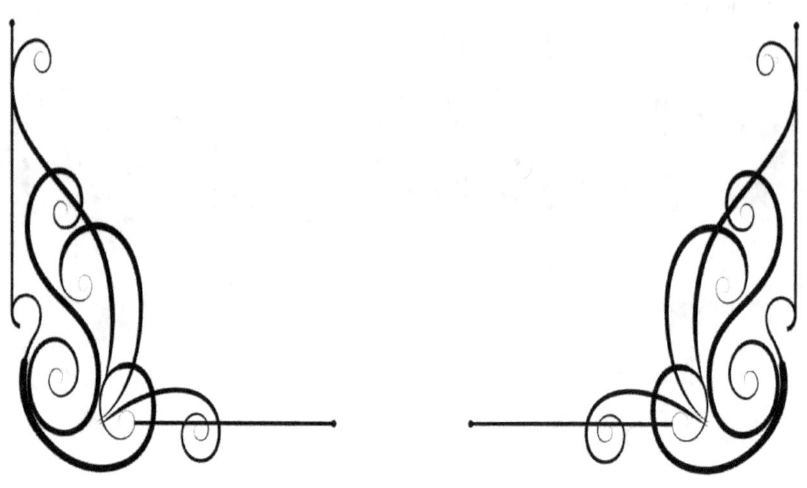

HOLD ONTO HOPE
DURING UNCERTAIN TIMES

Life won't always give you what you want. All you have to do is to glance at the headlines to see that we live in very uncertain times. The job you thought was safe might not be there tomorrow. The economy is up one day and down the next. There's always some natural disaster somewhere. And in the news, people seem to be more cruel than kind.

It's easy to get caught up in a negative spiral of self-doubt and anxiety. How do you stay hopeful and positive when around you all you see are negative messages and fear?

1. Be here now.
By focusing on the present, you will find it easier to take a step back and act as an observer. By practicing mindfulness, you'll see you can enjoy the simple things in life, no matter how bad things may seem. All worries and fears of the unknown can melt away if you focus on the present. Look for things in your life for which you're grateful. Making mindfulness a daily habit helps make hope a habit too.

2. Look for ways to exhibit compassion and empathy.
Spreading hope needs to start somewhere. Begin with the one person you can control, yourself. By looking for opportunities to pay it forward through random acts of kindness, you then become the impetus for others to do the same. Your compassionate heart and ability to walk in another's shoes will be the guide to those around you. And even if it's not? You'll have at least changed one heart - your own.

3. Do something.
Without hope you become stagnant, preferring to hide from the world. If you find that's the case with yourself, then it's time to force yourself into action, even if you don't feel like it. Get out of the house. Call a friend and suggest an outing or go by yourself. Find a green space somewhere because these places have been found to create calm and contentment in those who spend even a few minutes there. The goal is to find a positive action and embrace it, whatever that might be. Pick up litter, hug a child, do something that makes you feel good inside, and there you will find hope blossoming.

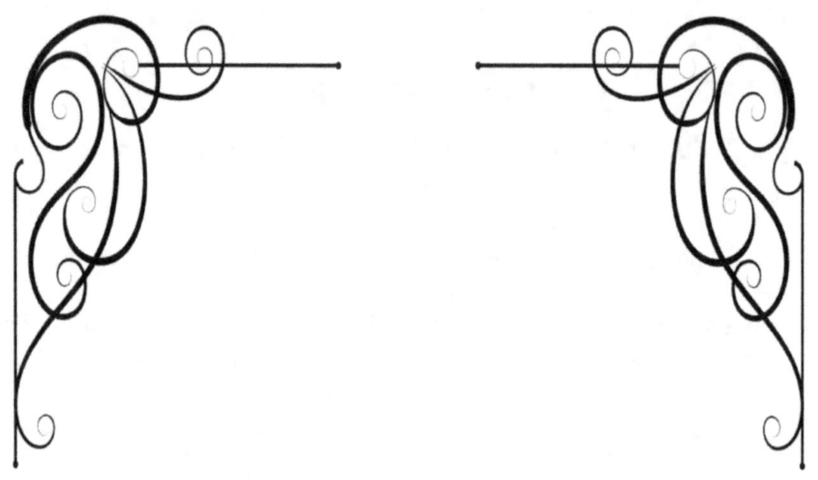

"Life is an uncertain game of chance; fate rolls the dice and you hope for the best."

~ Carol Stockall

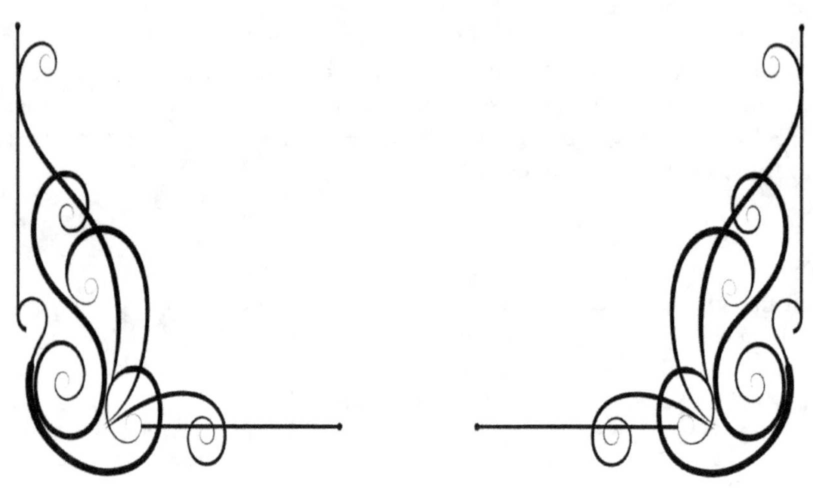

It's so easy to get caught up in the negativity of the world around you. Only by actively seeking hope will you find it. By practicing these three steps regularly, you'll find yourself able to look forward to each day, no matter what's going on around you.

Change is the only constant.

So remember:
- STAY IN THE PRESENT MOMENT
- PRACTICE RANDOM ACTS OF KINDNESS DAILY
- TAKE ACTION AND DO SOMETHING

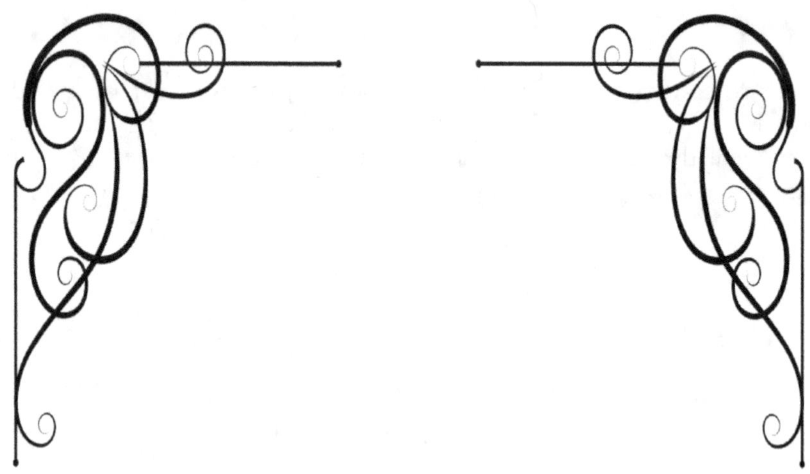

"Hope is the universal prescription for health."

~ Carol Stockall

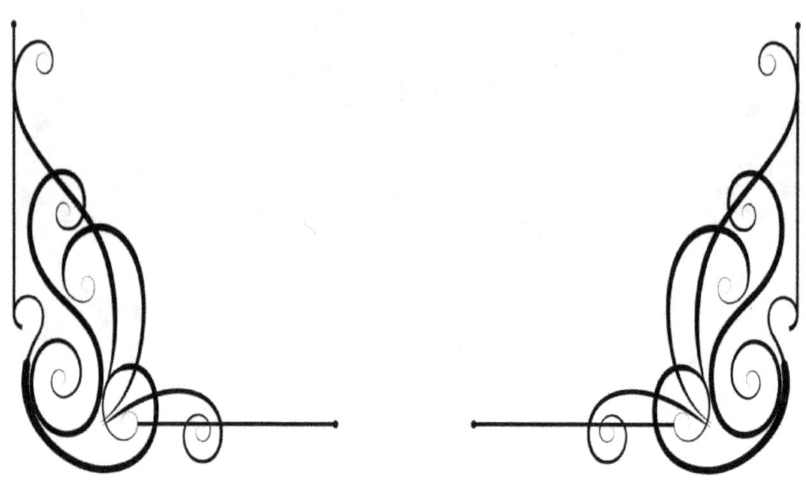

HOLD ONTO HOPE
DURING A HEALTH CRISIS

You probably already saw this coming. You hadn't been feeling well for a while, which then involved some trips to doctors and specialists. You had some tests, and you fell into that waiting game. By the time the doctor called, you were probably already losing hope. Now it's bad news, and you feel like your feet have just been knocked out from under you.

You have a lot of questions about treatment and what comes next. The hardest task? Don't stress, the doctor says. Don't lose hope.

Hope is probably the single most important part of your treatment plan. Studies have shown just how important it is for patients to have hope. Positive feelings about your diagnosis and the future will not only increase your chances of recovery and will also reduce that recovery time significantly.

So how do you keep hope alive when dealing with a health crisis?

1. Make a record of what's going on.
Journaling has been shown to improve mood significantly as it helps you put the entire illness in perspective and work through your feelings of what's going on. But as an added benefit, you'll also find that writing things down will help your doctors understand your symptoms and track the progress of the illness. By journaling, you create a more hopeful attitude and create a tool helpful to your recovery.

2. Put a firm focus on self-care.
When you're ill, you need to take care of yourself. It's surprising how many people still try to keep doing what they always have without taking time out to heal. You need to make sure you get plenty of rest and nutrition, but you need those treats that help to keep a positive attitude more than ever. So, enjoy that massage or splurge with that piece of chocolate cake. Indulging in little pleasures goes a long way toward keeping hope alive.

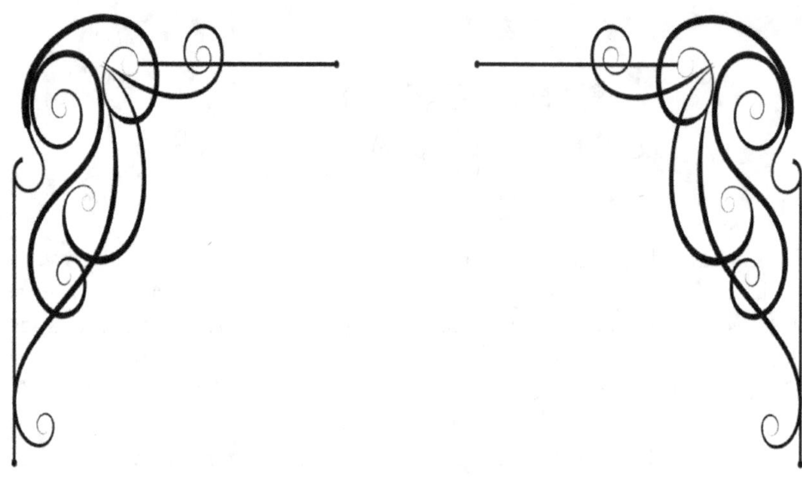

"Recovery from adversity requires healthy dose of hope."

~ Carol Stockall

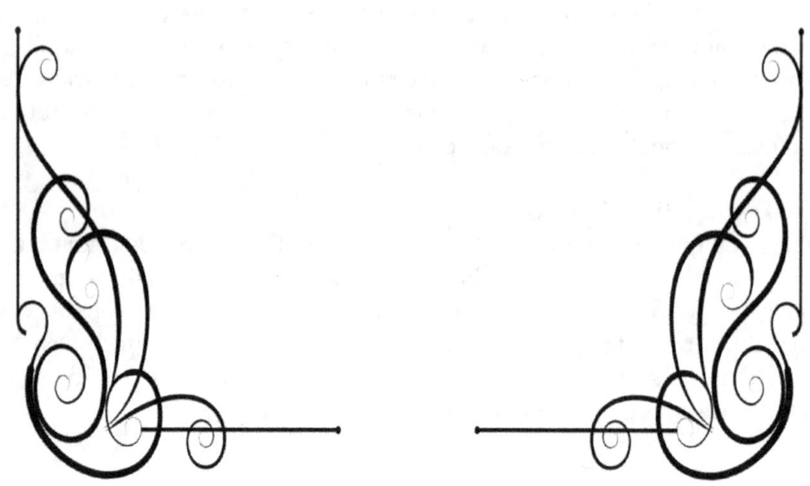

3.   Keep moving.

Research has proven that exercise affects your brain chemistry in positive ways. Hope thrives in that environment. Just make sure to follow your doctor's instructions and don't overdo it.

4.   Meditate.

Practicing mindfulness in the form of meditation, allows you to let go of the past and future. It can be challenging to live with the unknown and the fear of illness. Being in the moment even for a short time will ease the constant stress you may be experiencing during this difficult time.

Working to keep hope alive will help you on your health journey more than you think. With this hope, you'll find the needed energy and healing as you tread your path.

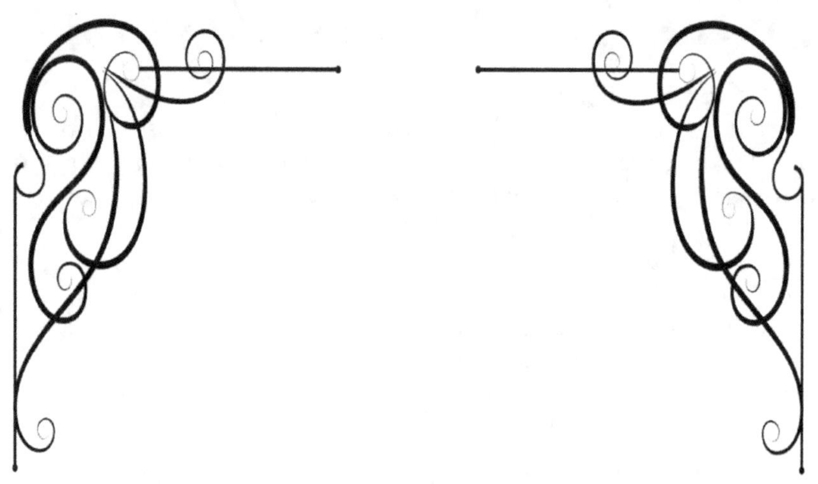

"When you hit a brick wall, hope helps you pick yourself up and move in a new direction."

~ Carol Stockall

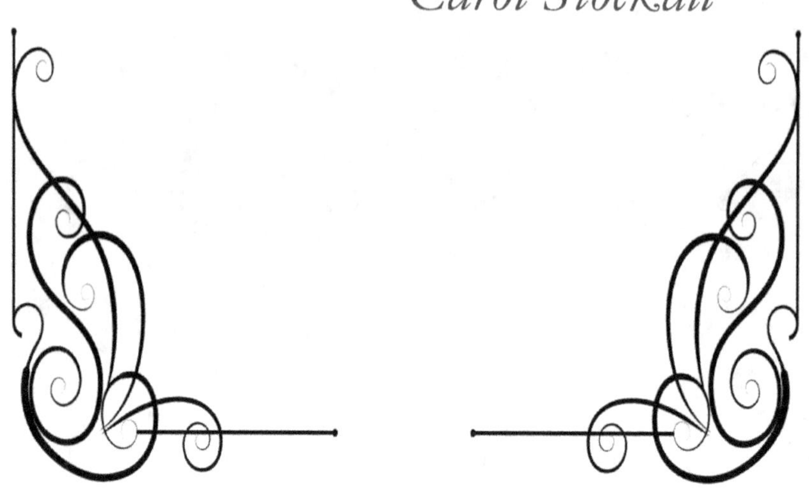

HOLD ONTO HOPE
WHILE YOU ARE OUT OF WORK

It wasn't supposed to be this hard. That last round of layoffs seemed to come out of nowhere, and now you're floundering. You've spent too many weeks of job hunting without any solid prospects on the horizon and are losing hope. Think of this as an opportunity to explore new types of work. You may even find different work that you would never have discovered. You might even find work that you love.

Without hope, you're never going to find that next job and get back to work. Hope is what's going to drag you up out of bed and get you to send out another dozen applications. Hope is how you're going to get through yet another interview. And hope is what's going to keep you going until you're safely employed again. Hope helps you look for work and love the work you find.

How? By taking action on these five practical tips:

1. Keep in the routine.
Keeping to a routine becomes incredibly important to your mental health when you're out of work. Start each day by getting dressed right down to your shoes and treat your life at home like work. Sit down at the computer and take care of the day's tasks, whether that means filling out applications, working on your resume, or researching job leads. This routine tells your body that you're still 'working' and does wonders for building hope.

2. Learn new skills.
Rather than sitting around waiting for the phone to ring, spend your time learning new skills. It's a great time to gain that certification or learn a new computer language. Learning puts you in a more hopeful frame of mind, and you can make your resume look even more impressive.

3. Escape the house.
It's easy to become hopeless when you're staring at the same four walls. Get out, talk to people, network. Even just going for a walk in the park will give you a change of scenery that will encourage a more positive, hopeful mindset.

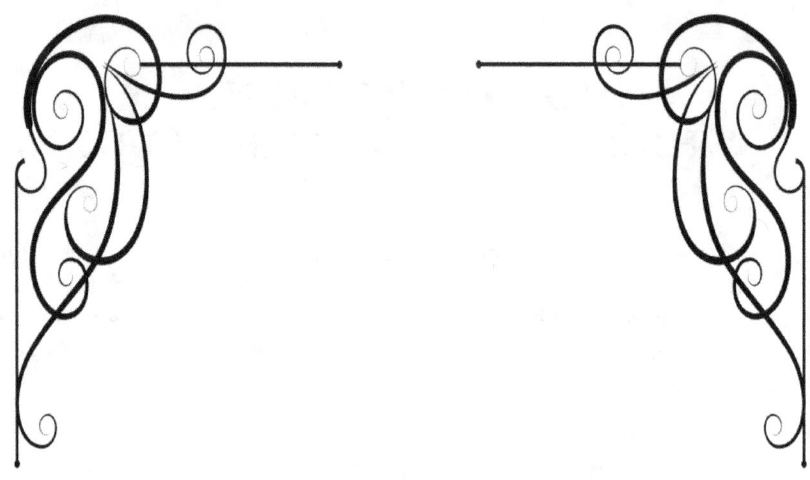

"When one door closes, hope
gives you the faith to keep
knocking on new ones."

~ Carol Stockall

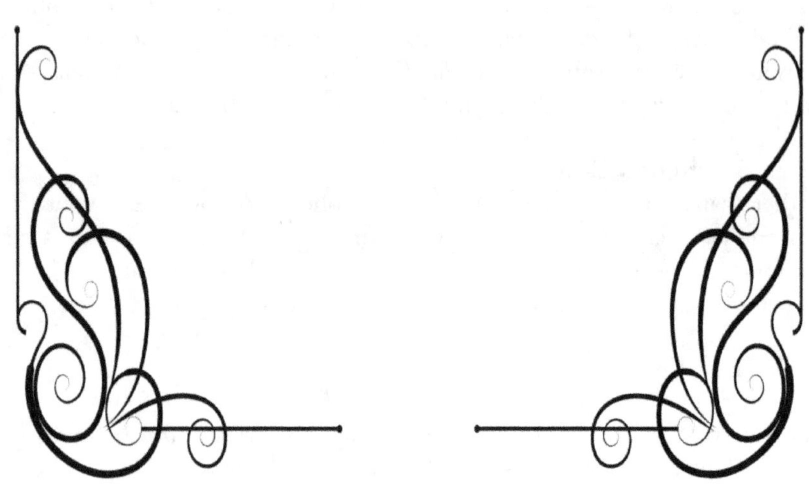

4.   Practice self-care.

When you neglect yourself, depression and hopelessness can move in and take over. During this stressful time, it's essential that you eat correctly, exercise well, and get enough sleep. Taking care of yourself is more important than ever when you are under a lot of stress. Feeling at your best will keep your hope of finding a great new job alive.

5.   Realize you're not the first and you won't be the last.

Remember that others have been in your position and found a job just fine. Look for the role models to help keep that hope alive. Talk to friends who have gone through a job loss. They may be able to give you some tips for finding your next job. Even if they don't, it will feel amazing to get some of the worries off your chest. Seek our support. Ask for help.

By focusing on positive action, you can keep hope alive even during the hardest job search. What's great about hope is that it's the impetus that's going to get you there. With hope, you're sure to be employed sooner than you think possible.

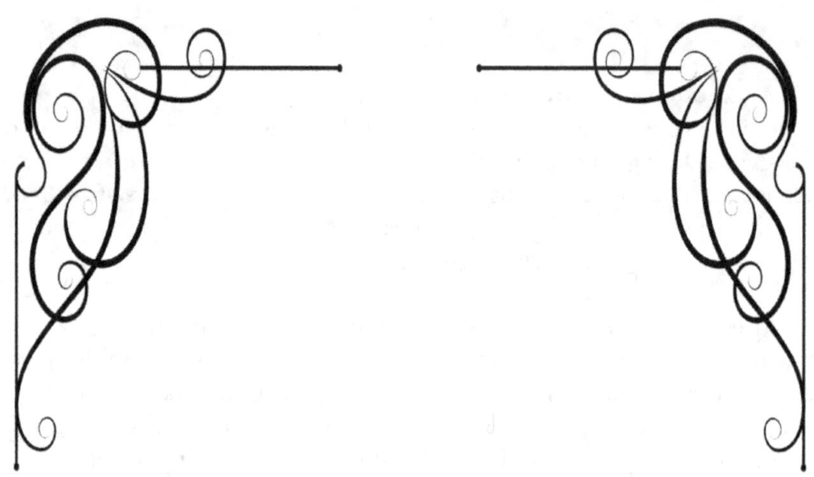

"Hope is the phoenix that wings her way from the ashes of despair to the flames of fortune."

~ Carol Stockall

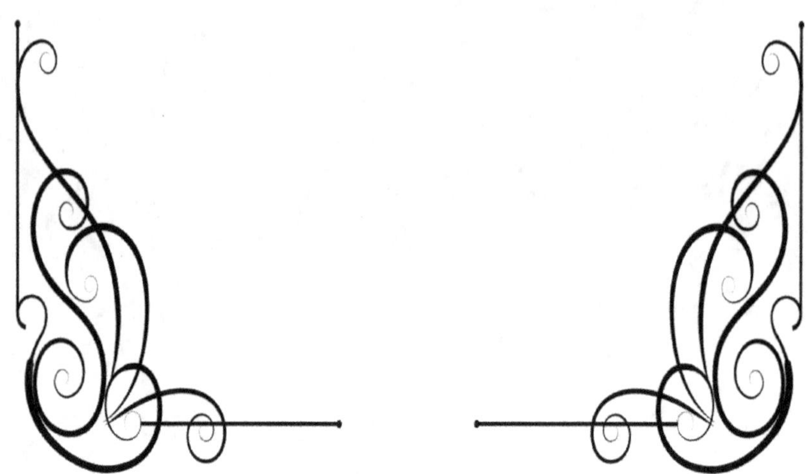

HOLD ONTO HOPE
WHILE BATTLING AGAINST BURNOUT

In the beginning this was your dream job. You loved your work and you worked hard. The passion for your profession was on fire. Over time that fire was doused by constant overload, overwhelm and exhaustion until you find yourself teetering on the edge of burnout. Or maybe you find yourself lying in the ashes of Now you're finding that being on stress leave is even more stressful because of the worry of returning to work.

Burnout is a real problem and it affects many people. Burnout is debilitating and it has become a leading cause for disability claims. In fact, burnout is so common it has become a growing global epidemic with billions in global economic costs. Even worse is the huge cost of human suffering. Here are some tips to help you hold onto hope if you are battling against burnout.

1.   Learn When It Happens
Recognize the signs of burnout so that if it does happen to you, there are steps to take to lighten the impact. Even better, knowing the signs of burnout can help you avoid them to begin with.

2.   Don't Concentrate Too Much Energy on Other People's Problems
Are you someone who is always trying to help others with their problems? Maybe, you are the go-to person when situations happen. It's good to help people but doing it too much can overwhelm you. When you experience other peoples' problems, it can get to you after a while. This is a common situation in healthcare and other industries where helping people is the job.

If it starts to affect your life, you will lose your ability to help others. Sometimes, it's best just to take a break in some way. Better to take a break than have a breakdown.

3.   Neglecting Your Own Problems
Along the same lines of helping others, neglecting your own problems is not going to make them go away. You need to deal with your situations promptly whenever possible. If you let them build up, they will contribute

to your burning out. Keep your own affairs in order before helping others.

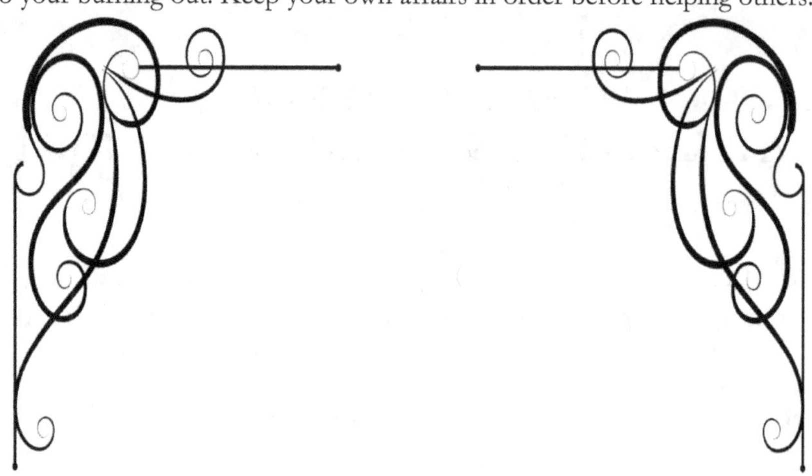

"When your passion and compassion begin to dwindle, hope is the spark that rekindles your flame."

~ Carol Stockall

4.   Exercise

It's proven that exercise reduces stress. Stress is a major cause of burnout. They go hand in hand. Frequent exercise will help you deal with your situations in an easier manner. This will reduce your chances of sickness and disease as well, which can be quite stressful.

5.   Goals

If you are just winging it at your job, you will never be able to tell if you are doing a good job. You'll also try to take on too much which is a major cause of burnout. By having goals, you set up expectations as to what you need to get done. It's probably a good idea to go over your goals with your manager to make sure he or she is on board.

6.   Change Careers

Over time, the career you choose will get stale, no matter what you try to do to revive it. If this continues for some time, it may be time to consider a new path. Instead of putting all of your energy into trying to make your stale career work, getting into something new can be just what you need.

7.   Socialize

We are social creatures. We need to be with others and not just at work. If you find the onset of burnout, consider getting out more and meet people or hook up with people you already know.

Burnout can be beaten. Remember burnout is a temporary state of being not a permanent character trait. These tips will give to the hope to persevere and help you bounce back even better.

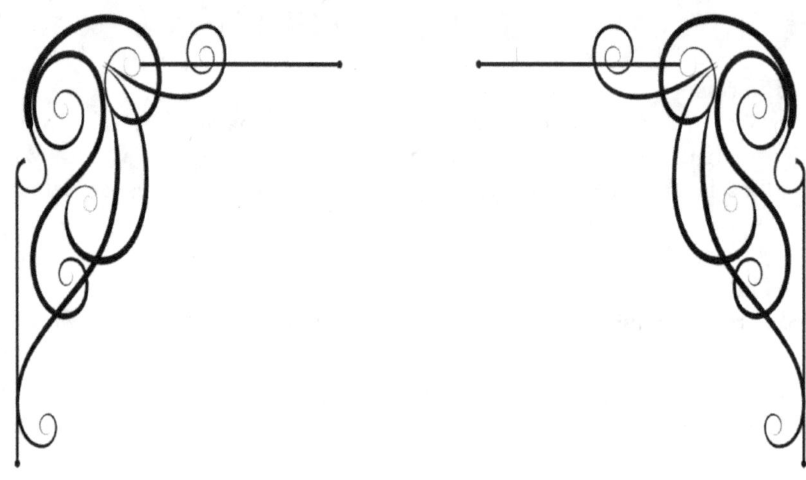

"If you're short on cash stay
long on hope."

~ Carol Stockall

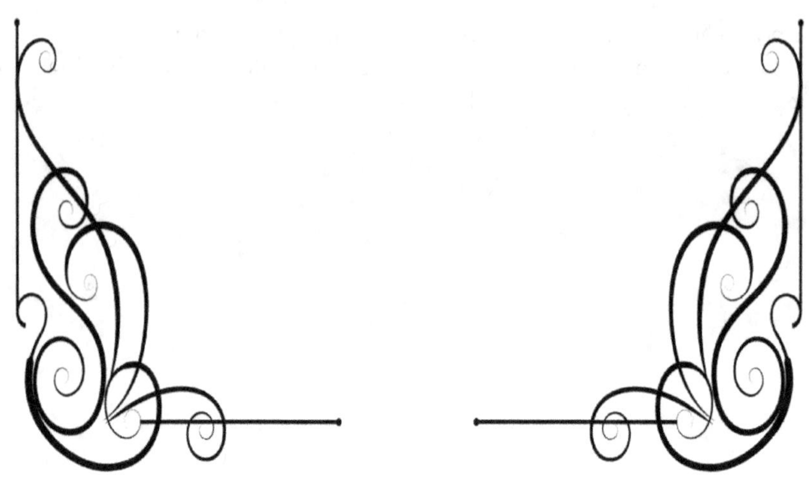

HOLD ONTO HOPE
WHILE FACING A FINANCIAL CRISIS

There are few things more stressful than a financial crisis. So much so that it's considered the number one reason that couples fight and is one of the leading causes of divorce. It can be a challenge to keep hope alive when facing a financial crisis, but it's not impossible. Try these five ways to jumpstart hope.

1. Be thankful for the things you do have.

When money worries begin, it's easy to get caught up in what you don't have instead of remembering what you do. Take a minute and give thanks for the people in your life. You should express gratitude for every good thing you can find, from your health to the beautiful flowers in your garden. Expressing gratitude takes the focus off of the negative and makes it easier to see the light at the end of the tunnel. Regardless of how bad things look, you still have many things for which to be thankful. Focus on those.

2. Get on a schedule.

Whenever things get stressed, maintaining some semblance of routine puts a measure of control back into your day. That allows you to turn your energy on solving the problem at hand. Routine then becomes the framework by which you organize your day. As a bonus, you'll find it's easier to find hope in structure than chaos.

3. Practice self-care.

Neglecting your health is a sure sign of hopelessness, creating a negative spiral that will send you down to the very depths of despair. That's why it's so important to keep eating correctly, exercising well, and getting adequate sleep. Feeling unwell will only add to the stress of your current financial situation.

4. Set manageable goals.

When you set too many goals, it's easy to become overwhelmed. When we're overwhelmed, we can give up hope and stop trying to make things better. Take care as you work to solve your financial problems so you create small, manageable goals that you can work on in small increments. Accomplishing goals leads to a feeling of well-being that in turn creates a hope that you will overcome the current crisis.

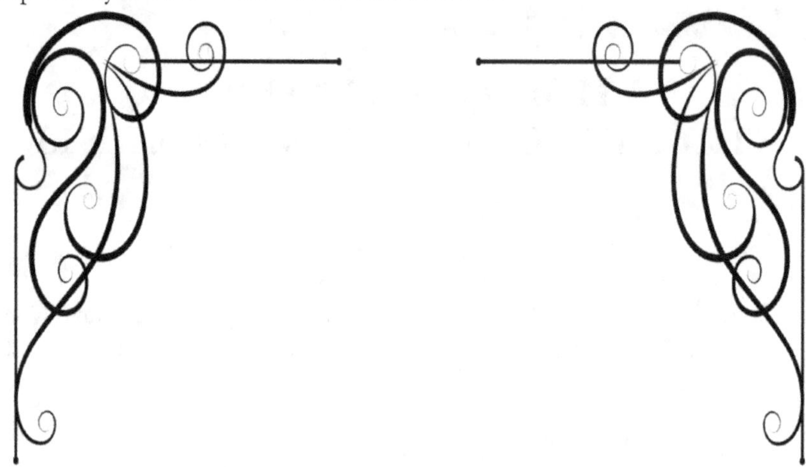

"Hope has the ability to transform scarcity into abundance."

~ Carol Stockall

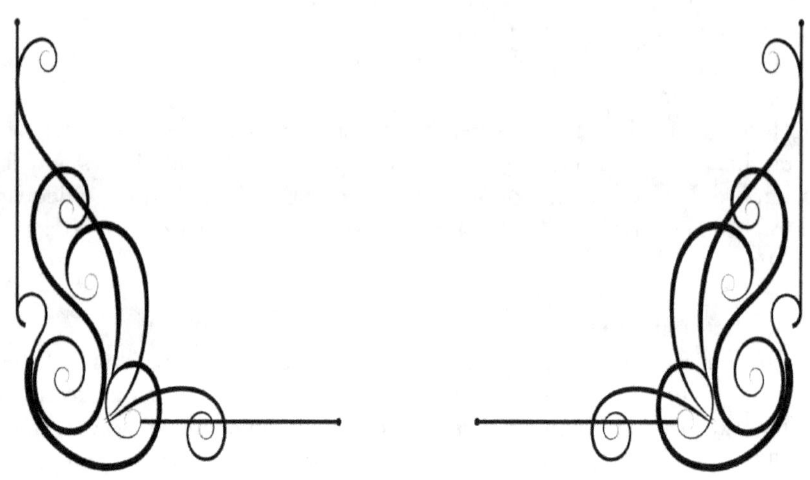

5. Look for beauty.

Embracing art and experiences, you find beautiful restores your soul. Thankfully, you can do quite a bit with very little money and a lot of creativity. Pick flowers, listen to a symphony online, create something beautiful. Hope thrives when we open ourselves to appreciating and creating beauty.

Finding hope during a financial crisis is hard, but not impossible. The main thing is to keep a positive outlook as you work on the problem. Having hope can help turn things around.

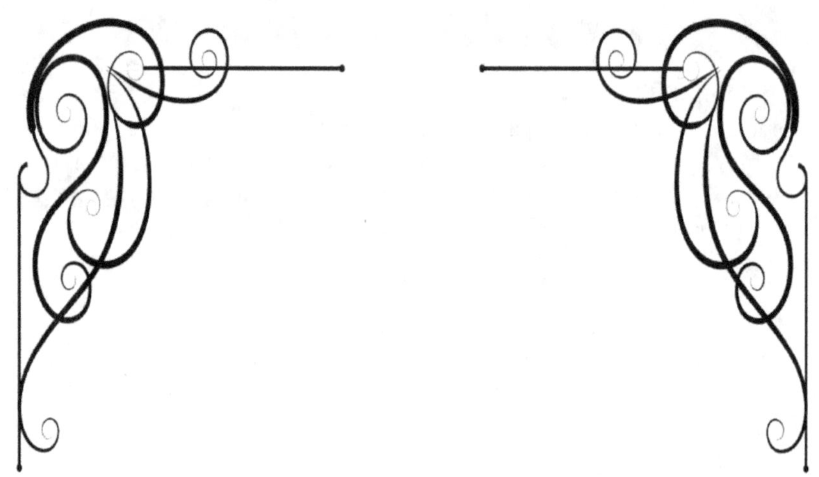

"Hope allows you create
graceful endings and gives you
the grit to make beginnings."

~ Carol Stockall

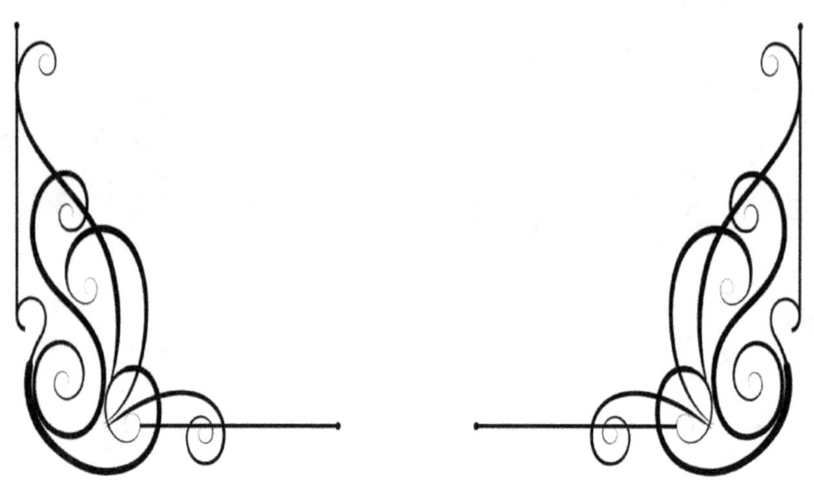

HOLD ONTO HOPE
AFTER DIVORCE

Divorce can be devastating. Life in the wake of divorce is complicated. The disruptive effects of divorce can permeate every aspect life. Divorce can literally turn your whole world upside-down. While you are in the process of uncoupling you are trying to navigate the world as a single person. Previously you were used to going through everything as one of a pair. Now, you might be floundering a little bit as you readjust to things. A little hope here would certainly go a long way.

So how do you find hope when your life feels like a disaster area?

1.   Accept the new status quo.

Like it or not, things have changed. A divorce has only made final what's probably been brewing for a long time. Accepting the situation means that you can move on and start the healing process. Hope comes with the realization that 'different' isn't always a bad thing.

2.   Realize that it does take two.

You cannot move past this moment without accepting that there were problems in your relationship for which you were at least partially responsible. Taking ownership of these issues and then letting go is a powerful tool that you can use to help work through the hopelessness that can settle after a divorce.

More importantly, hopelessness usually comes in thinking that the divorce was entirely out of your control. You might be afraid that another relationship would go the same way. Accepting that you did things in the marriage that led to this moment, you also see where you fell on the job. That gives you lessons to learn from, so your next relationship will turn out better.

3.   Stay in the moment.

By practicing mindfulness, you won't get so caught up in the past that led to this point. It doesn't give you room to worry about the future either. Living in the present allows you to enjoy the small things in life, pulling hope back into your heart.

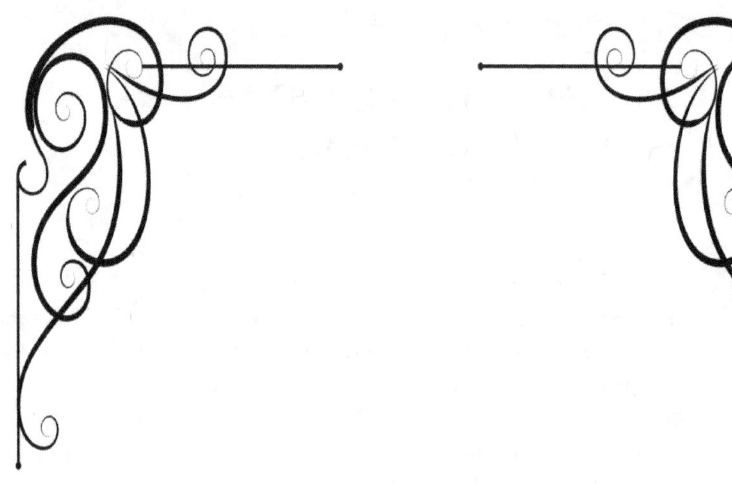

*"Fill your heart with hope
and then let hope fill your
heart with love."*

~ Carol Stockall

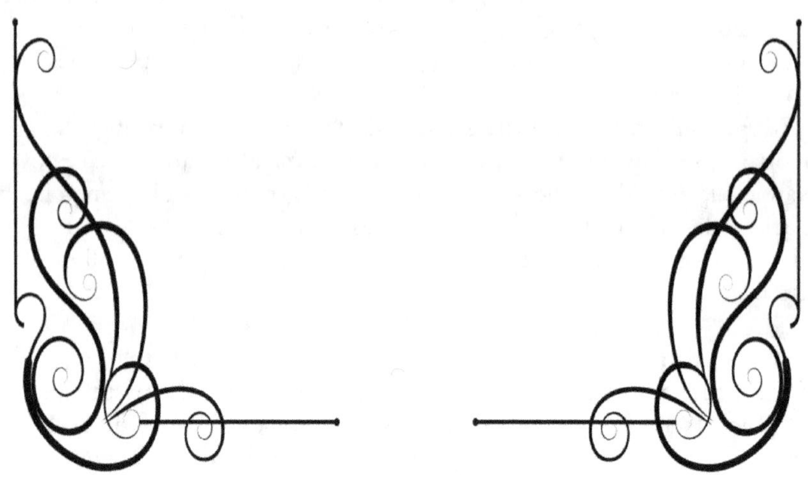

4.   Realize that this is a beginning and not an end.
Where do you go from here? Anywhere you like. Hope resurfaces with the realization that your life starts from this point, brand new and just waiting to see where you go with it. Now is your chance to go back to school, change jobs, or whatever you need to build a new life. Look for the opportunities, and realize that every time you take one, you are encouraging more hope in your life.

Life after divorce can be a time for a lot of hope if you only allow it back into your life. It's a time to let go of the past and everything that came before. The future is yours and is waiting for you to take charge of it.

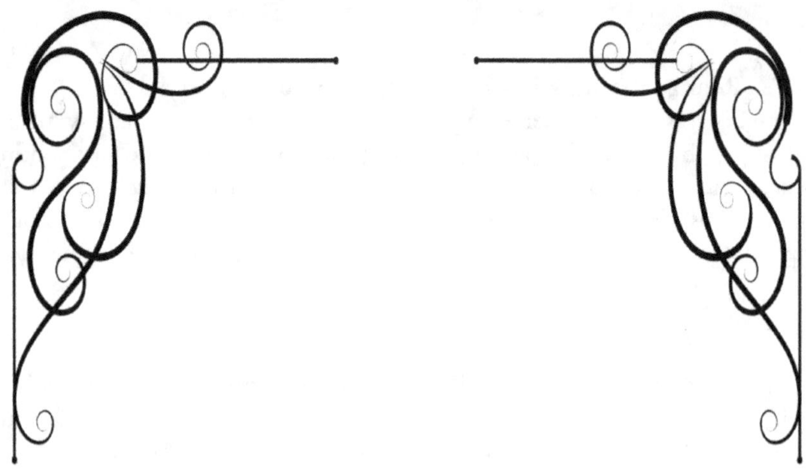

"Hope makes the impossible possible."

~ Carol Stockall

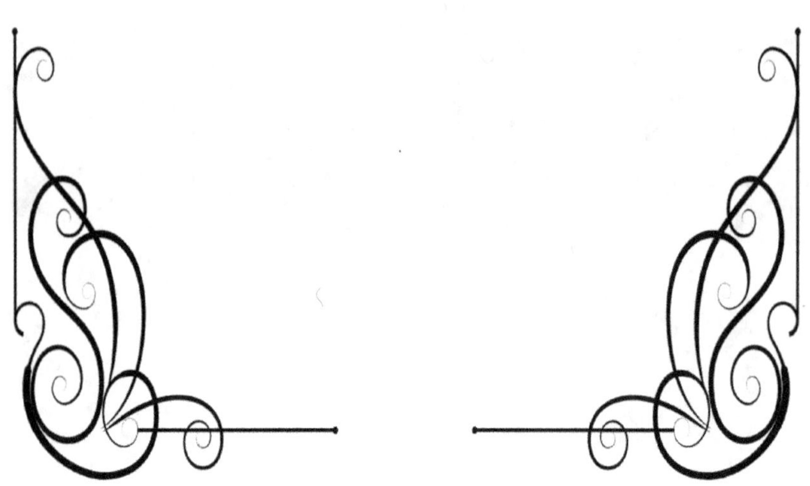

HOLD ONTO HOPE NO MATTER WHAT

Has despair become a regular specter in your life? Are you being haunted by negativity and paralyzed by a lack of motivation to reach your goals? Are you feeling like you're never going to catch up, much less get ahead? Perhaps you are facing something you prayed you'd never have to and finding a way forward seems impossible.

What you need is hope so you can hang on through this rough time. Hope is the expectation that good things can happen and then sets about to make sure they do. Hope is the motivation that puts you on the path toward turning your life around. To help you get started, below are five ways you can create a more hopeful life starting now.

1. Do a daily check-in.
How are you feeling? If you're not feeling hopeful, then it's time to ask yourself why. Take the time to journal about your feelings and allow yourself to look deeply on what is causing your despair. After you've gotten your worries and fears on paper, decide on one thing can you do now to experience a glimmer of hope? Do it!

2. Positively deal with your health.
The rules are simple. Eat right. Exercise. Sleep enough hours at night. When you're not taking care of yourself, and you don't feel well, it's easy to fall into a spiral of depression and self-doubt. It's when you feel great physically that hope thrives. What do you need to do to bring back hope then?

3. Know how to deal with stress.
There are a lot of simple ways to process negative emotion. Exercise, meditation, or taking some special "you" time by having a massage or taking a bubble bath can do wonders to boost hopefulness.

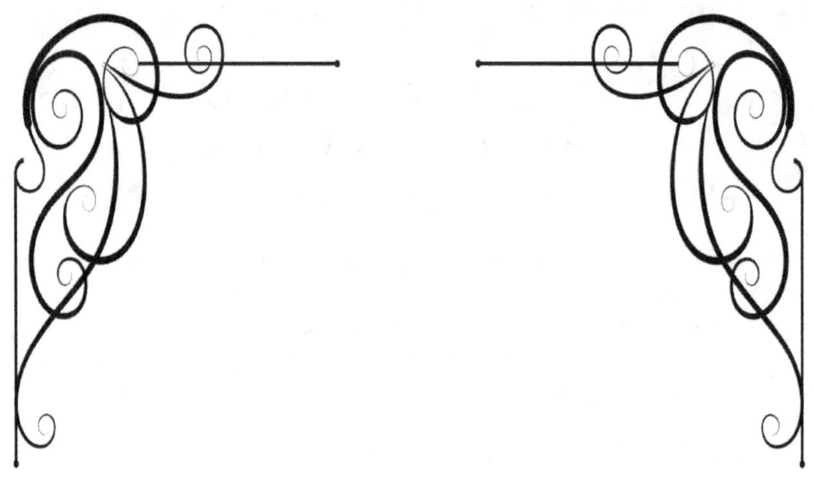

"Hope is magical, it gives
you the grit to never give up,
no matter what."

~ Carol Stockall

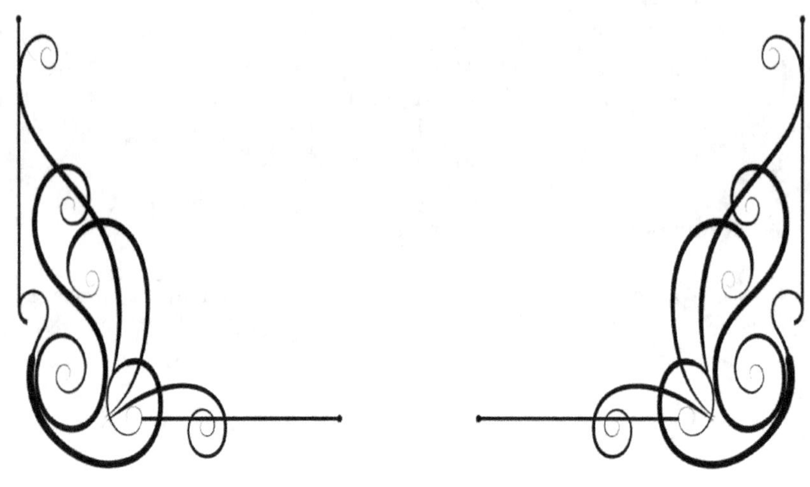

4. Surround yourself with hope.

Have positive people in your life. That may require you to say goodbye to some friends who bring you down, but it will be worth it. When you start focusing on all the good in your life, hope will naturally rebound. Because we are most influenced by the people we spend the most time with, it's imperative we replace the sad sacks in our lives with people who live life to the fullest.

5. Put the focus outside of yourself.

Ask how you can instill hope in the world around you? Pay it forward. Give compliments. Perform random acts of kindness. By acting in a hopeful manner, you wind up giving hope to those around you, who in turn share that hope with the world around them. The best way to ensure hopefulness is to share it with others.

Hope gives you the strength to hang on and the courage to keep going forward. Hope gives you the grit to never give up. Hope can transform your misery into magic.

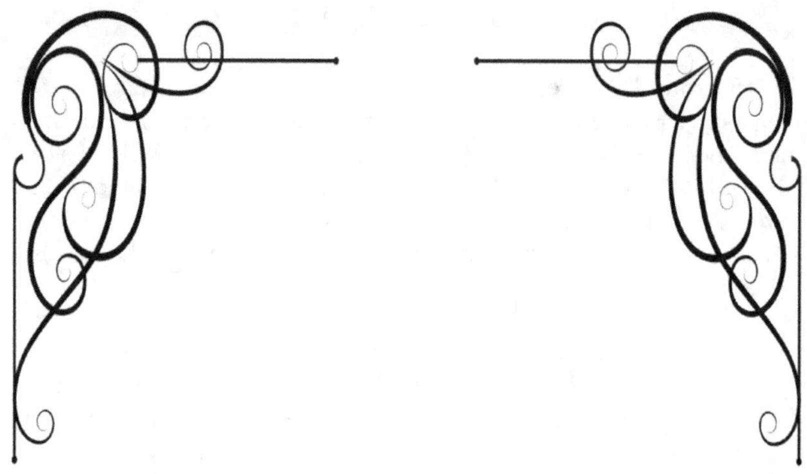

"Hope believes in miracles."

~ Carol Stockall

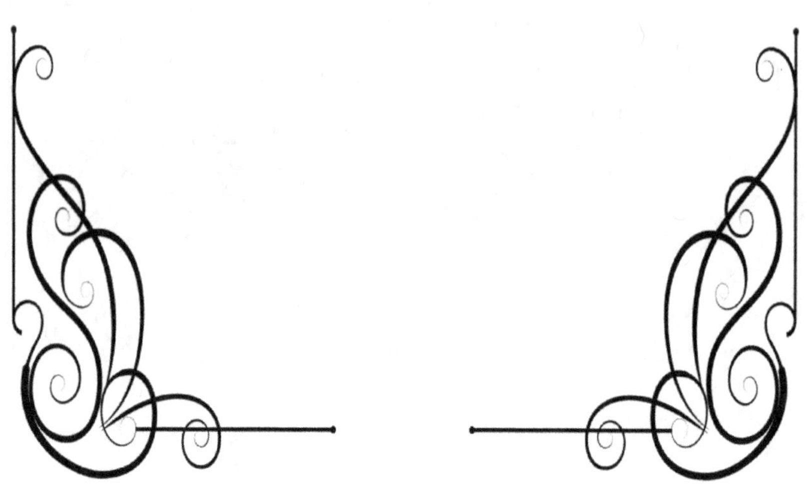

TIPS TO HOLD ONTO HOPE

1. Accept that sometimes things go wrong.
2. Reach out to your support system.
3. Let go of what you cannot change.
4. Look for the lesson in every struggle.
5. Keep a daily gratitude journal.
6. Learn to embrace uncertainty.
7. Focus on things you can control.
8. Tap into your faith and spirituality.
9. Recall how you overcame past struggles.
10. Find the courage to keep going.
11. Be grateful for everything you have.
12. Find things to look forward to.
13. Accept support and love from friends.
14. Ask for help.
15. Look for a silver lining in every struggle.
16. Try bringing hope to someone else.
17. Keep a log of all your successes.
18. Take care of yourself.
19. Use your passion as your guide.
20. Think outside-of-the-box.
21. Forgive others and forgive yourself.
22. Look for the good in others.
23. Start a meditation practice.
24. Journal about your hopes and dreams.
25. Spend time in nature.
26. Don't skip out on exercise.
27. Eat healthy and stay strong.
28. Nourish yourself with enough sleep.
29. Be bold.
30. Try something new.

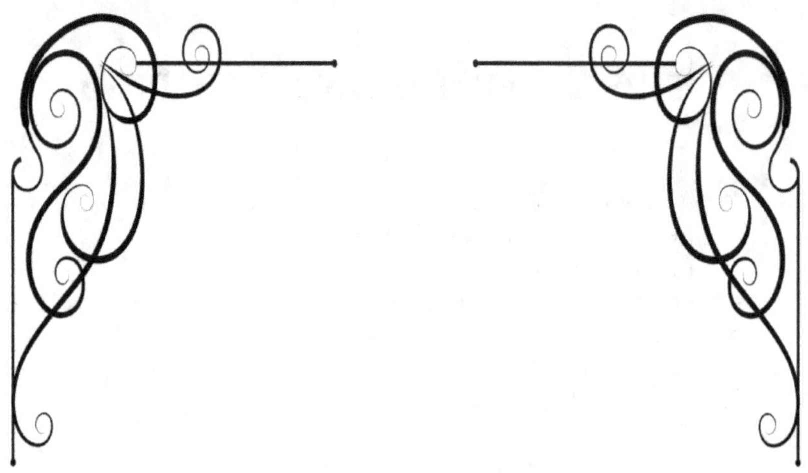

"Hope opens the portals of
possibility."

~ Carol Stockall

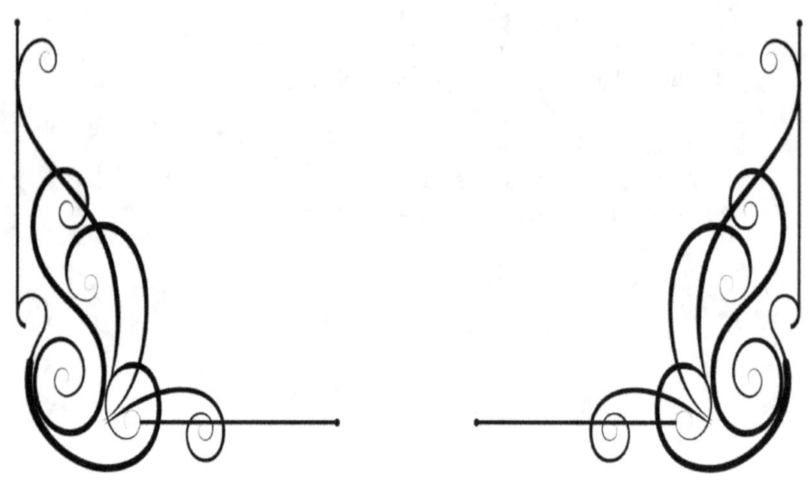

ABOUT THE AUTHOR

People often search for solutions during times of suffering. Carol has firsthand experience seeking solutions for the suffering of her patients, her clients and herself. Hope is always her first step in healing suffering.

Carol Stockall is a caregiver who has worn many hats. She began as a candy-striper, and later became a nurse, doctor, coach and counselor. A lifelong learner, Carol has a host of academic and professional letters behind her name including; BA, RN, MD, FRCPC, ACC, MC, and CCC. With decades of professional health care experience combined with a lifetime of personal experience Carol has earned a "PhD in life" that only comes with experience.

Today Carol's most known for her work coaching and counseling caregivers. She is a professional coach, certified by Erickson Coaching International, the International Coach Federation and the Physician Coaching Institute. Carol holds a post-degree diploma in Interprofessional Mental Health and a Master's degree in Counseling. Her thesis work was focused on burnout with a special interest in mindfulness to build balance and restore resilience.

Carol is dedicated to helping people hold onto hope and live out their life dreams. Get Carol's FREE JOURNAL to help you hold onto hope, download it here now https://carol-stockall.squarespace.com/s/Hold-Onto-Hope-Journal.pdf.

Use the journal as a companion to the book and jot down notes as you read. Then you'll be on your way to a brighter future.

To connect with Carol, visit her website at www.CarolStockall.com. Carol offers coaching and counseling for caregivers. Whether you are a caregiver in your home or at work connect with Carol and explore her list of helpful resources to help you hold onto hope.

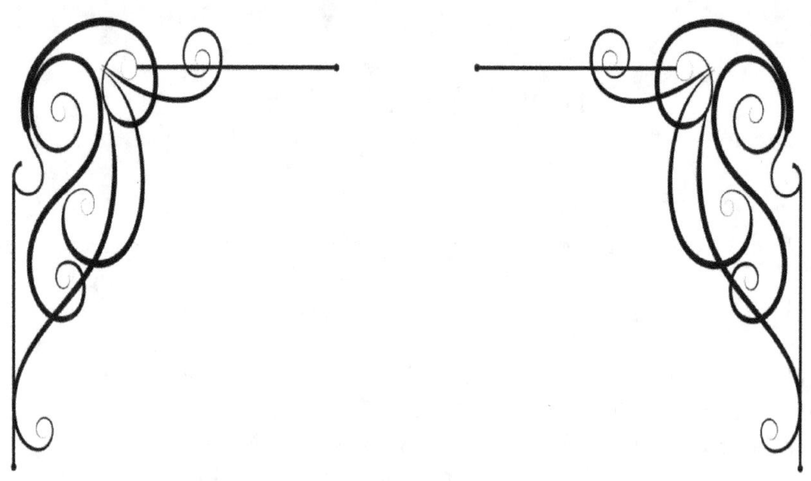

"When you feel like quitting hope helps you remember why you started."

~ Carol Stockall

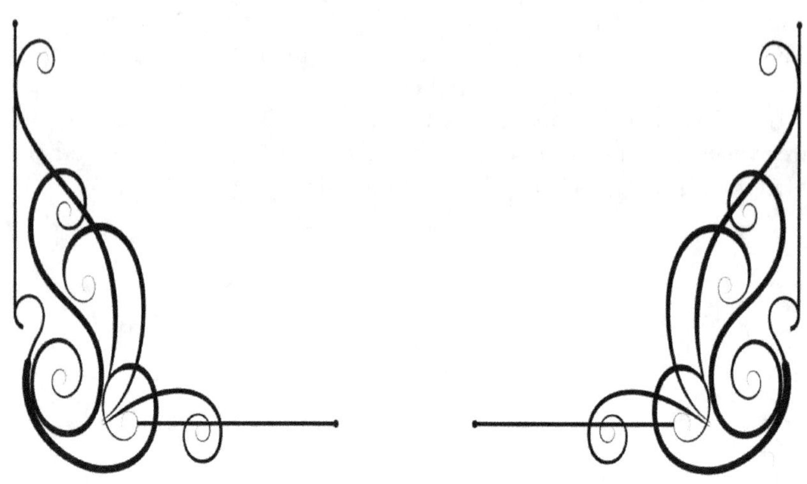